LEGEND:

 Meeting

 Hobby

 Sport

 Health

Name

Phone

E-Mail

	1	2	3	4	5	6	7	8	8	9	10	11	12	13	14
JAN															
FEB															
MARCH															
APRIL															
MAY															
JUNE															
JULY															
AUG															
SEPT															
OCT															
NOV															
DEC															

15	16	17	18	19	20	21	22	23	24	25	26	27	28	29	30	31

1

Celebrate
EVERY SINGLE
Day

Notes
What not to forget, what to remember

2
Thursday

3
Friday

MO	TU	WE	TH	FR	SA	SU
			1	2	3	4	5
6	7	8	9	10	11	12
13	14	15	16	17	18	19
20	21	22	23	24	25	26
27	28	29	30	31		

THAT'S *important* **THIS** *week*

4
Saturday

5
Sunday

MO	○	○	○	○
TU	○	○	○	○
WE	○	○	○	○
TH	○	○	○	○
FR	○	○	○	○
SA	○	○	○	○
SU	○	○	○	○

6
Monday

7
Tuesday

8
Wednesday

Notes
What not to forget, what to remember

9
Thursday

10
Friday

MO	TU	WE	TH	FR	SA	SU
		1	2	3	4	5
6	7	8	9	10	11	12
13	14	15	16	17	18	19
20	21	22	23	24	25	26
27	28	29	30	31		

THAT'S *important* THIS *week*

11
Saturday

12
Sunday

	○	○	○	○
MO	○	○	○	○
TU	○	○	○	○
WE	○	○	○	○
TH	○	○	○	○
FR	○	○	○	○
SA	○	○	○	○
SU	○	○	○	○

13
Monday

14
Tuesday

15
Wednesday

Notes
What not to forget, what to remember

16
Thursday

17
Friday

18
Saturday

19
Sunday

MO	TU	WE	TH	FR	SA	SU
		1	2	3	4	5
6	7	8	9	10	11	12
13	14	15	16	17	18	19
20	21	22	23	24	25	26
27	28	29	30	31		

THAT'S *important* THIS *week*

MO
TU
WE
TH
FR
SA
SU

20
Monday

21
Tuesday

22
Wednesday

Notes
What not to forget, what to remember

23
Thursday

24
Friday

MO	TU	WE	TH	FR	SA	SU
			1	2	3	4	5
6	7	8	9	10	11	12
13	14	15	16	17	18	19
20	21	22	23	24	25	26
27	28	29	30	31		

THAT'S *important*
THIS *week*

25
Saturday

26
Sunday

MO	○	○	○	○
TU	○	○	○	○
WE	○	○	○	○
TH	○	○	○	○
FR	○	○	○	○
SA	○	○	○	○
SU	○	○	○	○

27
Monday

28
Tuesday

29
Wednesday

Notes
What not to forget, what to remember

30
Thursday

31
Friday

MO	TU	WE	TH	FR	SA	SU
		1	2	3	4	5
6	7	8	9	10	11	12
13	14	15	16	17	18	19
20	21	22	23	24	25	26
27	28	29	30	31		

THAT'S *important*
THIS *week*

Hello
February

FOR A GREAT MONTH

Notes
What not to forget, what to remember

MO	TU	WE	TH	FR	SA	SU
					1	2
3	4	5	6	7	8	9
10	11	12	13	14	15	16
17	18	19	20	21	22	23
24	25	26	27	28	29	

THAT'S *important* THIS *week*

1
Saturday

2
Sunday

MO	○	○	○	○
TU	○	○	○	○
WE	○	○	○	○
TH	○	○	○	○
FR	○	○	○	○
SA	○	○	○	○
SU	○	○	○	○

3
Monday

4
Tuesday

5
Wednesday

Notes
What not to forget, what to remember

6
Thursday

7
Friday

MO	TU	WE	TH	FR	SA	SU
					1	2
3	4	5	6	7	8	9
10	11	12	13	14	15	16
17	18	19	20	21	22	23
24	25	26	27	28	29	

THAT'S *important* THIS *week*

8
Saturday

9
Sunday

	○	○	○	○
MO	○	○	○	○
TU	○	○	○	○
WE	○	○	○	○
TH	○	○	○	○
FR	○	○	○	○
SA	○	○	○	○
SU	○	○	○	○

10
Monday

11
Tuesday

12
Wednesday

Notes
What not to forget, what to remember

13
Thursday

14
Friday

15
Saturday

16
Sunday

MO	TU	WE	TH	FR	SA	SU
					1	2
3	4	5	6	7	8	9
10	11	12	13	14	15	16
17	18	19	20	21	22	23
24	25	26	27	28	29	

THAT'S *important* THIS *week*

MO	◯	◯	◯	◯
TU	◯	◯	◯	◯
WE	◯	◯	◯	◯
TH	◯	◯	◯	◯
FR	◯	◯	◯	◯
SA	◯	◯	◯	◯
SU	◯	◯	◯	◯

17
Monday

18
Tuesday

19
Wednesday

Notes
What not to forget, what to remember

20
Thursday

21
Friday

22
Saturday

23
Sunday

MO	TU	WE	TH	FR	SA	SU
					1	2
3	4	5	6	7	8	9
10	11	12	13	14	15	16
17	18	19	20	21	22	23
24	25	26	27	28	29	

THAT'S *important* THIS *week*

MO	○	○	○	○
TU	○	○	○	○
WE	○	○	○	○
TH	○	○	○	○
FR	○	○	○	○
SA	○	○	○	○
SU	○	○	○	○

24
Monday

25
Tuesday

26
Wednesday

Notes
What not to forget, what to remember

27
Thursday

28
Friday

MO	TU	WE	TH	FR	SA	SU
					1	2
3	4	5	6	7	8	9
10	11	12	13	14	15	16
17	18	19	20	21	22	23
24	25	26	27	28	29	

THAT'S *important*
THIS *week*

29
Saturday

MO	○	○	○	○
TU	○	○	○	○
WE	○	○	○	○
TH	○	○	○	○
FR	○	○	○	○
SA	○	○	○	○
SU	○	○	○	○

MONTH MARCH

Time for Now !

LET THE MOMENTS HAVE THEIR SPACE.

Notes

What not to forget, what to remember

March

2020

MO	TU	WE	TH	FR	SA	SU
						1
2	3	4	5	6	7	8
9	10	11	12	13	14	15
16	17	18	19	20	21	22
23	24	25	26	27	28	29
30	31					

THAT'S *important* THIS *week*

_____

_____

_____

_____

1
Sunday

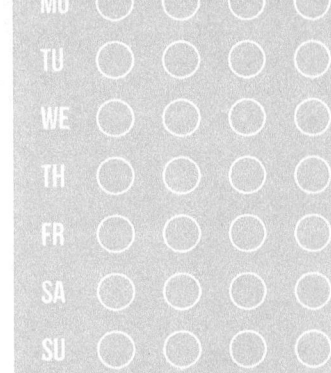

	💬	☕	🏋	❤
MO	○	○	○	○
TU	○	○	○	○
WE	○	○	○	○
TH	○	○	○	○
FR	○	○	○	○
SA	○	○	○	○
SU	○	○	○	○

2
Monday

3
Tuesday

4
Wednesday

Notes
What not to forget, what to remember

5
Thursday

6
Friday

March
2020

MO	TU	WE	TH	FR	SA	SU
						1
2	3	4	5	6	7	8
9	10	11	12	13	14	15
16	17	18	19	20	21	22
23	24	25	26	27	28	29
30	31					

THAT'S *important* **THIS** *week*

7
Saturday

8
Sunday

MO	○	○	○	○
TU	○	○	○	○
WE	○	○	○	○
TH	○	○	○	○
FR	○	○	○	○
SA	○	○	○	○
SU	○	○	○	○

9
Monday

10
Tuesday

11
Wednesday

Notes
What not to forget, what to remember

12
Thursday

13
Friday

14
Saturday

15
Sunday

MO	TU	WE	TH	FR	SA	SU
						1
2	3	4	5	6	7	8
9	10	11	12	13	14	15
16	17	18	19	20	21	22
23	24	25	26	27	28	29
30	31					

THAT'S *important* THIS *week*

MO	○ ○	○ ○	○ ○
TU	○ ○	○ ○	○ ○
WE	○ ○	○ ○	○ ○
TH	○ ○	○ ○	○ ○
FR	○ ○	○ ○	○ ○
SA	○ ○	○ ○	○ ○
SU	○ ○	○ ○	○ ○

16
Monday

17
Tuesday

18
Wednesday

Notes
What not to forget, what to remember

19
Thursday

20
Friday

21
Saturday

22
Sunday

March
2020

MO	TU	WE	TH	FR	SA	SU
						1
2	3	4	5	6	7	8
9	10	11	12	13	14	15
16	17	18	19	20	21	22
23	24	25	26	27	28	29
30	31					

THAT'S *important* THIS *week*

MO	○	○	○	○
TU	○	○	○	○
WE	○	○	○	○
TH	○	○	○	○
FR	○	○	○	○
SA	○	○	○	○
SU	○	○	○	○

23
Monday

24
Tuesday

25
Wednesday

Notes
What not to forget, what to remember

26
Thursday

27
Friday

MO	TU	WE	TH	FR	SA	SU
						1
2	3	4	5	6	7	8
9	10	11	12	13	14	15
16	17	18	19	20	21	22
23	24	25	26	27	28	29
30	31					

THAT'S *important* THIS *week*

28
Saturday

29
Sunday

MO	○	○	○	○
TU	○	○	○	○
WE	○	○	○	○
TH	○	○	○	○
FR	○	○	○	○
SA	○	○	○	○
SU	○	○	○	○

30
Monday

31
Tuesday

Notes
What not to forget, what to remember

March

2020

MO	TU	WE	TH	FR	SA	SU
						1
2	3	4	5	6	7	8
9	10	11	12	13	14	15
16	17	18	19	20	21	22
23	24	25	26	27	28	29
30	31					

THAT'S *important* THIS *week*

Look back:

DID APRIL DO WHAT YOU WANT?

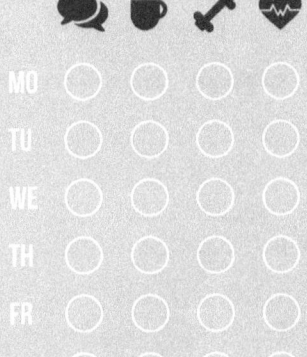

MO	○	○	○	○
TU	○	○	○	○
WE	○	○	○	○
TH	○	○	○	○
FR	○	○	○	○
SA	○	○	○	○
SU	○	○	○	○

Now

April

NO KIDDING! THIS WILL BE YOUR MONTH!

Notes
What not to forget, what to remember

2
Thursday

3
Friday

MO	TU	WE	TH	FR	SA	SU
		1	2	3	4	5
6	7	8	9	10	11	12
13	14	15	16	17	18	19
20	21	22	23	24	25	26
27	28	29	30			

THAT'S *important* THIS *week*

4
Saturday

5
Sunday

	💬	☕	🏋	❤
MO	◯	◯	◯	◯
TU	◯	◯	◯	◯
WE	◯	◯	◯	◯
TH	◯	◯	◯	◯
FR	◯	◯	◯	◯
SA	◯	◯	◯	◯
SU	◯	◯	◯	◯

6
Monday

7
Tuesday

8
Wednesday

Notes
What not to forget, what to remember

9
Thursday

10
Friday

11
Saturday

12
Sunday

MO	TU	WE	TH	FR	SA	SU
		1	2	3	4	5
6	7	8	9	10	11	12
13	14	15	16	17	18	19
20	21	22	23	24	25	26
27	28	29	30			

THAT'S *important* THIS *week*

MO	○	○	○	○
TU	○	○	○	○
WE	○	○	○	○
TH	○	○	○	○
FR	○	○	○	○
SA	○	○	○	○
SU	○	○	○	○

13
Monday

14
Tuesday

15
Wednesday

Notes
What not to forget, what to remember

16
Thursday

17
Friday

MO	TU	WE	TH	FR	SA	SU
		1	2	3	4	5
6	7	8	9	10	11	12
13	14	15	16	17	18	19
20	21	22	23	24	25	26
27	28	29	30			

THAT'S *important* THIS *week*

18
Saturday

19
Sunday

	💬	☕	🏋	💗
MO	○	○	○	○
TU	○	○	○	○
WE	○	○	○	○
TH	○	○	○	○
FR	○	○	○	○
SA	○	○	○	○
SU	○	○	○	○

20
Monday

21
Tuesday

22
Wednesday

Notes
What not to forget, what to remember

23
Thursday

24
Friday

25
Saturday

26
Sunday

MO	TU	WE	TH	FR	SA	SU
		1	2	3	4	5
6	7	8	9	10	11	12
13	14	15	16	17	18	19
20	21	22	23	24	25	26
27	28	29	30			

THAT'S *important* THIS *week*

	💬	☕	🏋	💓
MO	◯	◯	◯	◯
TU	◯	◯	◯	◯
WE	◯	◯	◯	◯
TH	◯	◯	◯	◯
FR	◯	◯	◯	◯
SA	◯	◯	◯	◯
SU	◯	◯	◯	◯

27
Monday

28
Tuesday

29
Wednesday

Notes
What not to forget, what to remember

30
Thursday

MO	TU	WE	TH	FR	SA	SU
		1	2	3	4	5
6	7	8	9	10	11	12
13	14	15	16	17	18	19
20	21	22	23	24	25	26
27	28	29	30			

THAT'S *important* THIS *week*

A NEW START AT EACH END...

SIMPLY CONTINUE..

	💬	☕	🏋	💓
MO	◯	◯	◯	◯
TU	◯	◯	◯	◯
WE	◯	◯	◯	◯
TH	◯	◯	◯	◯
FR	◯	◯	◯	◯
SA	◯	◯	◯	◯
SU	◯	◯	◯	◯

May

EVERY SINGLE CALENDAR PAGE A NEW CHANCE ...

Use it!

Notes

What not to forget, what to remember

1
Friday

May
2020

MO	TU	WE	TH	FR	SA	SU
				1	2	3
4	5	6	7	8	9	10
11	12	13	14	15	16	17
18	19	20	21	22	23	24
25	26	27	28	29	30	31

THAT'S *important*
THIS *week*

2
Saturday

3
Sunday

	💬	☕	🏋	❤
MO	○	○	○	○
TU	○	○	○	○
WE	○	○	○	○
TH	○	○	○	○
FR	○	○	○	○
SA	○	○	○	○
SU	○	○	○	○

4
Monday

5
Tuesday

6
Wednesday

Notes
What not to forget, what to remember

7
Thursday

8
Friday

9
Saturday

10
Sunday

MO	TU	WE	TH	FR	SA	SU
				1	2	3
4	5	6	7	8	9	10
11	12	13	14	15	16	17
18	19	20	21	22	23	24
25	26	27	28	29	30	31

THAT'S *important* THIS *week*

MO

TU

WE

TH

FR

SA

SU

11
Monday

12
Tuesday

13
Wednesday

Notes
What not to forget, what to remember

14
Thursday

15
Friday

May
2020

MO	TU	WE	TH	FR	SA	SU
				1	2	3
4	5	6	7	8	9	10
11	12	13	14	15	16	17
18	19	20	21	22	23	24
25	26	27	28	29	30	31

THAT'S *important* THIS *week*

16
Saturday

17
Sunday

MO	○	○	○	○
TU	○	○	○	○
WE	○	○	○	○
TH	○	○	○	○
FR	○	○	○	○
SA	○	○	○	○
SU	○	○	○	○

18
Monday

19
Tuesday

20
Wednesday

Notes
What not to forget, what to remember

21
Thursday

22
Friday

23
Saturday

24
Sunday

MO	TU	WE	TH	FR	SA	SU
				1	2	3
4	5	6	7	8	9	10
11	12	13	14	15	16	17
18	19	20	21	22	23	24
25	26	27	28	29	30	31

THAT'S *important* THIS *week*

MO
TU
WE
TH
FR
SA
SU

25
Monday

26
Tuesday

27
Wednesday

Notes
What not to forget, what to remember

28
Thursday

29
Friday

MO	TU	WE	TH	FR	SA	SU
				1	2	3
4	5	6	7	8	9	10
11	12	13	14	15	16	17
18	19	20	21	22	23	24
25	26	27	28	29	30	31

THAT'S *important* THIS *week*

30
Saturday

31
Sunday

	💬	☕	🏋	❤
MO	○	○	○	○
TU	○	○	○	○
WE	○	○	○	○
TH	○	○	○	○
FR	○	○	○	○
SA	○	○	○	○
SU	○	○	○	○

1
Monday

2
Tuesday

3
Wednesday

Notes
What not to forget, what to remember

4
Thursday

5
Friday

MO	TU	WE	TH	FR	SA	SU
1	2	3	4	5	6	7
8	9	10	11	12	13	14
15	16	17	18	19	20	21
22	23	24	25	26	27	28
29	30					

THAT'S *important*
THIS *week*

6
Saturday

7
Sunday

	💬	☕	🏋	❤
MO	○	○	○	○
TU	○	○	○	○
WE	○	○	○	○
TH	○	○	○	○
FR	○	○	○	○
SA	○	○	○	○
SU	○	○	○	○

8
Monday

9
Tuesday

10
Wednesday

Notes
What not to forget, what to remember

11
Thursday

12
Friday

MO	TU	WE	TH	FR	SA	SU
1	2	3	4	5	6	7
8	9	10	11	12	13	14
15	16	17	18	19	20	21
22	23	24	25	26	27	28
29	30					

THAT'S *important*
THIS *week*

13
Saturday

14
Sunday

MO
TU
WE
TH
FR
SA
SU

15
Monday

16
Tuesday

17
Wednesday

Notes
What not to forget, what to remember

18
Thursday

19
Friday

20
Saturday

21
Sunday

Jun.
2020

MO	TU	WE	TH	FR	SA	SU
1	2	3	4	5	6	7
8	9	10	11	12	13	14
15	16	17	18	19	20	21
22	23	24	25	26	27	28
29	30					

THAT'S *important* **THIS** *week*

MO	○	○	○	○
TU	○	○	○	○
WE	○	○	○	○
TH	○	○	○	○
FR	○	○	○	○
SA	○	○	○	○
SU	○	○	○	○

22
Monday

23
Tuesday

24
Wednesday

Notes
What not to forget, what to remember

25
Thursday

26
Friday

27
Saturday

28
Sunday

MO	TU	WE	TH	FR	SA	SU
1	2	3	4	5	6	7
8	9	10	11	12	13	14
15	16	17	18	19	20	21
22	23	24	25	26	27	28
29	30					

THAT'S *important* THIS *week*

MO	◯	◯	◯	◯
TU	◯	◯	◯	◯
WE	◯	◯	◯	◯
TH	◯	◯	◯	◯
FR	◯	◯	◯	◯
SA	◯	◯	◯	◯
SU	◯	◯	◯	◯

29
Monday

30
Tuesday

Notes
What not to forget, what to remember

If you
SNOOZE,
you lose!

MO	TU	WE	TH	FR	SA	SU
1	2	3	4	5	6	7
8	9	10	11	12	13	14
15	16	17	18	19	20	21
22	23	24	25	26	27	28
29	30					

THAT'S *important* THIS *week*

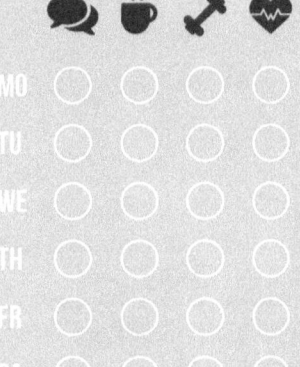

	💬	☕	🏋	❤
MO	◯	◯	◯	◯
TU	◯	◯	◯	◯
WE	◯	◯	◯	◯
TH	◯	◯	◯	◯
FR	◯	◯	◯	◯
SA	◯	◯	◯	◯
SU	◯	◯	◯	◯

A cheerful

„HELLO SUNSHINE!“

Starting in July

Notes
What not to forget, what to remember

2
Thursday

3
Friday

MO	TU	MI	TH	FR	SA	SU
		1	2	3	4	5
6	7	8	9	10	11	12
13	14	15	16	17	18	19
20	21	22	23	24	25	26
27	28	29	30	31		

THAT'S *important* THIS *week*

4
Saturday

5
Sunday

	💬	☕	🏋	❤
MO	○	○	○	○
TU	○	○	○	○
MI	○	○	○	○
TH	○	○	○	○
FR	○	○	○	○
SA	○	○	○	○
SU	○	○	○	○

6
Monday

7
Tuesday

8
Wednesday

Notes
What not to forget, what to remember

9
Thursday

10
Friday

MO	TU	MI	TH	FR	SA	SU
		1	2	3	4	5
6	7	8	9	10	11	12
13	14	15	16	17	18	19
20	21	22	23	24	25	26
27	28	29	30	31		

THAT'S *important*
THIS *week*

11
Saturday

12
Sunday

MO	○	○	○	○
TU	○	○	○	○
MI	○	○	○	○
TH	○	○	○	○
FR	○	○	○	○
SA	○	○	○	○
SU	○	○	○	○

13
Monday

14
Tuesday

15
Wednesday

Notes
What not to forget, what to remember

16
Thursday

17
Friday

MO	TU	MI	TH	FR	SA	SU
		1	2	3	4	5
6	7	8	9	10	11	12
13	14	15	16	17	18	19
20	21	22	23	24	25	26
27	28	29	30	31		

THAT'S *important* THIS *week*

18
Saturday

19
Sunday

MO	○	○	○	○
TU	○	○	○	○
MI	○	○	○	○
TH	○	○	○	○
FR	○	○	○	○
SA	○	○	○	○
SU	○	○	○	○

20
Monday

21
Tuesday

22
Wednesday

Notes
What not to forget, what to remember

23
Thursday

24
Friday

MO	TU	MI	TH	FR	SA	SU
		1	2	3	4	5
6	7	8	9	10	11	12
13	14	15	16	17	18	19
20	21	22	23	24	25	26
27	28	29	30	31		

THAT'S *important* **THIS** *week*

25
Saturday

26
Sunday

	💬	☕	🏋	💓
MO	○	○	○	○
TU	○	○	○	○
MI	○	○	○	○
TH	○	○	○	○
FR	○	○	○	○
SA	○	○	○	○
SU	○	○	○	○

27
Monday

28
Tuesday

29
Wednesday

Notes
What not to forget, what to remember

30
Thursday

31
Friday

MO	TU	MI	TH	FR	SA	SU
		1	2	3	4	5
6	7	8	9	10	11	12
13	14	15	16	17	18	19
20	21	22	23	24	25	26
27	28	29	30	31		

THAT'S *important* THIS *week*

High Life

DAY AFTER DAY

MO	◯	◯	◯	◯
TU	◯	◯	◯	◯
MI	◯	◯	◯	◯
TH	◯	◯	◯	◯
FR	◯	◯	◯	◯
SA	◯	◯	◯	◯
SU	◯	◯	◯	◯

Hey! August
Midsummer Time!

THIS MONTH MAKES YOU SHINE

Notes
What not to forget, what to remember

SUMMER TIME!

Aug.
2020

MO	TU	WE	TH	FR	SA	SU
					1	2
3	4	5	6	7	8	9
10	11	12	13	14	15	16
17	18	19	20	21	22	23
24	25	26	27	28	29	30
31						

THAT'S *important* THIS *week*

_____

_____

_____

_____

MO	○	○	○	○
TU	○	○	○	○
WE	○	○	○	○
TH	○	○	○	○
FR	○	○	○	○
SA	○	○	○	○
SU	○	○	○	○

1
Saturday

2
Sunday

3
Monday

4
Tuesday

5
Wednesday

Notes
What not to forget, what to remember

6
Thursday

7
Friday

8
Saturday

9
Sunday

MO	TU	WE	TH	FR	SA	SU
					1	2
3	4	5	6	7	8	9
10	11	12	13	14	15	16
17	18	19	20	21	22	23
24	25	26	27	28	29	30
31						

THAT'S *important*
THIS *week*

MO	○	○	○	○
TU	○	○	○	○
WE	○	○	○	○
TH	○	○	○	○
FR	○	○	○	○
SA	○	○	○	○
SU	○	○	○	○

10
Monday

11
Tuesday

12
Wednesday

Notes
What not to forget, what to remember

13
Thursday

14
Friday

MO	TU	WE	TH	FR	SA	SU
					1	2
3	4	5	6	7	8	9
10	11	12	13	14	15	16
17	18	19	20	21	22	23
24	25	26	27	28	29	30
31						

THAT'S *important*
THIS *week*

15
Saturday

16
Sunday

MO	○	○	○	○
TU	○	○	○	○
WE	○	○	○	○
TH	○	○	○	○
FR	○	○	○	○
SA	○	○	○	○
SU	○	○	○	○

17
Monday

18
Tuesday

19
Wednesday

Notes
What not to forget, what to remember

20
Thursday

21
Friday

22
Saturday

23
Sunday

MO	TU	WE	TH	FR	SA	SU
					1	2
3	4	5	6	7	8	9
10	11	12	13	14	15	16
17	18	19	20	21	22	23
24	25	26	27	28	29	30
31						

THAT'S *important*
THIS *week*

MO	○	○	○	○
TU	○	○	○	○
WE	○	○	○	○
TH	○	○	○	○
FR	○	○	○	○
SA	○	○	○	○
SU	○	○	○	○

24
Monday

25
Tuesday

26
Wednesday

Notes
What not to forget, what to remember

27
Thursday

28
Friday

29
Saturday

30
Sunday

MO	TU	WE	TH	FR	SA	SU
					1	2
3	4	5	6	7	8	9
10	11	12	13	14	15	16
17	18	19	20	21	22	23
24	25	26	27	28	29	30
31						

THAT'S *important*
THIS *week*

MO				
TU				
WE				
TH				
FR				
SA				
SU				

31
Monday

Notes
What not to forget, what to remember

SUNFILLED AND FULL OF ENERGY YOU SET OFF TO THE

September!

MO	TU	WE	TH	FR	SA	SU
					1	2
3	4	5	6	7	8	9
10	11	12	13	14	15	16
17	18	19	20	21	22	23
24	25	26	27	28	29	30
31						

THAT'S *important* THIS *week*

_____

_____

_____

_____

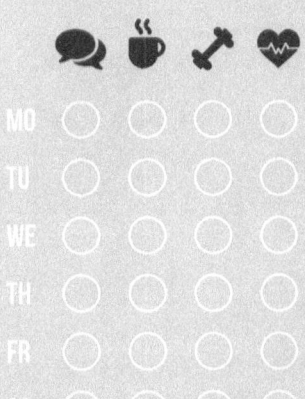

	💬	☕	🏋	💓
MO	○	○	○	○
TU	○	○	○	○
WE	○	○	○	○
TH	○	○	○	○
FR	○	○	○	○
SA	○	○	○	○
SU	○	○	○	○

1
Tuesday

2
Wednesday

Notes
What not to forget, what to remember

3
Thursday

4
Friday

5
Saturday

6
Sunday

MO	TU	WE	TH	FR	SA	SU
	1	2	3	4	5	6
7	8	9	10	11	12	13
14	15	16	17	18	19	20
21	22	23	24	25	26	27
28	29	30				

THAT'S *important* **THIS** *week*

MO
TU
WE
TH
FR
SA
SU

7
Monday

8
Tuesday

9
Wednesday

Notes
What not to forget, what to remember

10
Thursday

11
Friday

12
Saturday

13
Sunday

MO	TU	WE	TH	FR	SA	SU
	1	2	3	4	5	6
7	8	9	10	11	12	13
14	15	16	17	18	19	20
21	22	23	24	25	26	27
28	29	30				

THAT'S *important* THIS *week*

	💬	☕	🏋	💓
MO	○	○	○	○
TU	○	○	○	○
WE	○	○	○	○
TH	○	○	○	○
FR	○	○	○	○
SA	○	○	○	○
SU	○	○	○	○

14
Monday

15
Tuesday

16
Wednesday

Notes
What not to forget, what to remember

17
Thursday

18
Friday

MO	TU	WE	TH	FR	SA	SU
	1	2	3	4	5	6
7	8	9	10	11	12	13
14	15	16	17	18	19	20
21	22	23	24	25	26	27
28	29	30				

THAT'S *important* **THIS** *week*

19
Saturday

20
Sunday

	💬	☕	🏋	💓
MO	◯	◯	◯	◯
TU	◯	◯	◯	◯
WE	◯	◯	◯	◯
TH	◯	◯	◯	◯
FR	◯	◯	◯	◯
SA	◯	◯	◯	◯
SU	◯	◯	◯	◯

21
Monday

22
Tuesday

23
Wednesday

Notes
What not to forget, what to remember

24
Thursday

25
Friday

26
Saturday

27
Sunday

MO	TU	WE	TH	FR	SA	SU
	1	2	3	4	5	6
7	8	9	10	11	12	13
14	15	16	17	18	19	20
21	22	23	24	25	26	27
28	29	30				

THAT'S *important* THIS *week*

	○	○	○	○
MO	○	○	○	○
TU	○	○	○	○
WE	○	○	○	○
TH	○	○	○	○
FR	○	○	○	○
SA	○	○	○	○
SU	○	○	○	○

28
Monday

29
Tuesday

30
Wednesday

Notes
What not to forget, what to remember

Come On!

WHERE'S A WILL,
THERE'S A WAY.

MO	TU	WE	TH	FR	SA	SU
	1	2	3	4	5	6
7	8	9	10	11	12	13
14	15	16	17	18	19	20
21	22	23	24	25	26	27
28	29	30				

THAT'S *important* THIS *week*

_____

_____

_____

_____

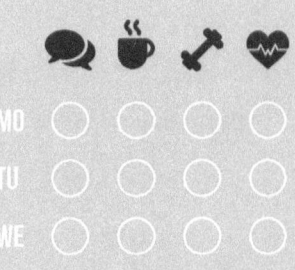

MO	◯	◯	◯	◯
TU	◯	◯	◯	◯
WE	◯	◯	◯	◯
TH	◯	◯	◯	◯
FR	◯	◯	◯	◯
SA	◯	◯	◯	◯
SU	◯	◯	◯	◯

LIFE IS A JOURNEY,

not a destination!

Notes
What not to forget, what to remember

1
Thursday

2
Friday

MO	TU	WE	TH	FR	SA	SU
			1	2	3	4
5	6	7	8	9	10	11
12	13	14	15	16	17	18
19	20	21	22	23	24	25
26	27	28	29	30	31	

THAT'S *important* THIS *week*

3
Saturday

4
Sunday

	💬	☕	🏋	♥
MO	○	○	○	○
TU	○	○	○	○
WE	○	○	○	○
TH	○	○	○	○
FR	○	○	○	○
SA	○	○	○	○
SU	○	○	○	○

5
Monday

6
Tuesday

7
Wednesday

Notes
What not to forget, what to remember

8
Thursday

9
Friday

10
Saturday

11
Sunday

MO	TU	WE	TH	FR	SA	SU
			1	2	3	4
5	6	7	8	9	10	11
12	13	14	15	16	17	18
19	20	21	22	23	24	25
26	27	28	29	30	31	

THAT'S *important* THIS *week*

MO	○	○	○	○
TU	○	○	○	○
WE	○	○	○	○
TH	○	○	○	○
FR	○	○	○	○
SA	○	○	○	○
SU	○	○	○	○

12
Monday

13
Tuesday

14
Wednesday

Notes
What not to forget, what to remember

15
Thursday

16
Friday

17
Saturday

18
Sunday

MO	TU	WE	TH	FR	SA	SU
			1	2	3	4
5	6	7	8	9	10	11
12	13	14	15	16	17	18
19	20	21	22	23	24	25
26	27	28	29	30	31	

THAT'S *important* THIS *week*

	💬	☕	🏋	❤
MO	○	○	○	○
TU	○	○	○	○
WE	○	○	○	○
TH	○	○	○	○
FR	○	○	○	○
SA	○	○	○	○
SU	○	○	○	○

19
Monday

20
Tuesday

21
Wednesday

Notes
What not to forget, what to remember

22
Thursday

23
Friday

24
Saturday

25
Sunday

MO	TU	WE	TH	FR	SA	SU
			1	2	3	4
5	6	7	8	9	10	11
12	13	14	15	16	17	18
19	20	21	22	23	24	25
26	27	28	29	30	31	

THAT'S *important* THIS *week*

MO	○	○	○	○
TU	○	○	○	○
WE	○	○	○	○
TH	○	○	○	○
FR	○	○	○	○
SA	○	○	○	○
SU	○	○	○	○

26
Monday

27
Tuesday

28
Wednesday

Notes
What not to forget, what to remember

29
Thursday

30
Friday

MO	TU	WE	TH	FR	SA	SU
			1	2	3	4
5	6	7	8	9	10	11
12	13	14	15	16	17	18
19	20	21	22	23	24	25
26	27	28	29	30	31	

THAT'S *important* THIS *week*

31
Saturday

MO	◯	◯	◯	◯
TU	◯	◯	◯	◯
WE	◯	◯	◯	◯
TH	◯	◯	◯	◯
FR	◯	◯	◯	◯
SA	◯	◯	◯	◯
SU	◯	◯	◯	◯

NOVEMBER

Be cool!

THE END OF THE YEAR IS APPROACHING - STEP ON THE GAS AGAIN.

Notes

What not to forget, what to remember

Nov.

2020

MO	TU	WE	TH	FR	SA	SU
						1
2	3	4	5	6	7	8
9	10	11	12	13	14	15
16	17	18	19	20	21	22
23	24	25	26	27	28	29
30						

THAT'S *important* THIS *week*

_____

_____

_____

1
Sunday

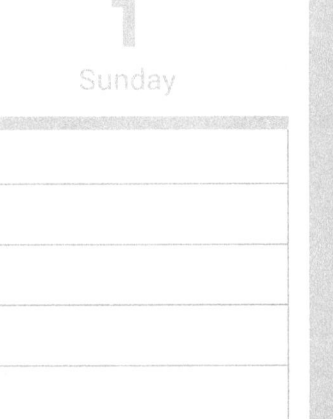

MO	◯	◯	◯	◯
TU	◯	◯	◯	◯
WE	◯	◯	◯	◯
TH	◯	◯	◯	◯
FR	◯	◯	◯	◯
SA	◯	◯	◯	◯
SU	◯	◯	◯	◯

2
Monday

3
Tuesday

4
Wednesday

Notes
What not to forget, what to remember

5
Thursday

6
Friday

MO	TU	WE	TH	FR	SA	SU
						1
2	3	4	5	6	7	8
9	10	11	12	13	14	15
16	17	18	19	20	21	22
23	24	25	26	27	28	29
30						

THAT'S *important* THIS *week*

7
Saturday

8
Sunday

	💬	☕	🏋	💓
MO	◯	◯	◯	◯
TU	◯	◯	◯	◯
WE	◯	◯	◯	◯
TH	◯	◯	◯	◯
FR	◯	◯	◯	◯
SA	◯	◯	◯	◯
SU	◯	◯	◯	◯

9
Monday

10
Tuesday

11
Wednesday

Notes
What not to forget, what to remember

12
Thursday

13
Friday

14
Saturday

15
Sunday

MO	TU	WE	TH	FR	SA	SU
						1
2	3	4	5	6	7	8
9	10	11	12	13	14	15
16	17	18	19	20	21	22
23	24	25	26	27	28	29
30						

THAT'S *important* THIS *week*

MO	○	○	○	○
TU	○	○	○	○
WE	○	○	○	○
TH	○	○	○	○
FR	○	○	○	○
SA	○	○	○	○
SU	○	○	○	○

16
Monday

17
Tuesday

18
Wednesday

Notes
What not to forget, what to remember

19
Thursday

20
Friday

21
Saturday

22
Sunday

MO	TU	WE	TH	FR	SA	SU
						1
2	3	4	5	6	7	8
9	10	11	12	13	14	15
16	17	18	19	20	21	22
23	24	25	26	27	28	29
30						

THAT'S *important* **THIS** *week*

MO
TU
WE
TH
FR
SA
SU

23
Monday

24
Tuesday

25
Wednesday

Notes
What not to forget, what to remember

26
Thursday

27
Friday

Nov.
2020

MO	TU	WE	TH	FR	SA	SU
						1
2	3	4	5	6	7	8
9	10	11	12	13	14	15
16	17	18	19	20	21	22
23	24	25	26	27	28	29
30						

THAT'S *important*
THIS *week*

28
Saturday

29
Sunday

MO	○	○	○	○
TU	○	○	○	○
WE	○	○	○	○
TH	○	○	○	○
FR	○	○	○	○
SA	○	○	○	○
SU	○	○	○	○

1
Tuesday

2
Wednesday

Notes
What not to forget, what to remember

3
Thursday

4
Friday

MO	TU	WE	TH	FR	SA	SU
	1	2	3	4	5	6
7	8	9	10	11	12	13
14	15	16	17	18	19	20
21	22	23	24	25	26	27
28	29	30	31			

THAT'S *important*
THIS *week*

5
Saturday

6
Sunday

	💬	☕	🏋	❤
MO	○	○	○	○
TU	○	○	○	○
WE	○	○	○	○
TH	○	○	○	○
FR	○	○	○	○
SA	○	○	○	○
SU	○	○	○	○

7
Monday

8
Tuesday

9
Wednesday

Notes
What not to forget, what to remember

10
Thursday

11
Friday

MO	TU	WE	TH	FR	SA	SU
	1	2	3	4	5	6
7	8	9	10	11	12	13
14	15	16	17	18	19	20
21	22	23	24	25	26	27
28	29	30	31			

THAT'S *important*
THIS *week*

12
Saturday

13
Sunday

	💬	☕	🏋	💓
MO	○	○	○	○
TU	○	○	○	○
WE	○	○	○	○
TH	○	○	○	○
FR	○	○	○	○
SA	○	○	○	○
SU	○	○	○	○

14
Monday

15
Tuesday

16
Wednesday

Notes
What not to forget, what to remember

17
Thursday

18
Friday

MO	TU	WE	TH	FR	SA	SU
	1	2	3	4	5	6
7	8	9	10	11	12	13
14	15	16	17	18	19	20
21	22	23	24	25	26	27
28	29	30	31			

THAT'S *important* **THIS** *week*

19
Saturday

20
Sunday

	💬	☕	🏋	💓
MO	◯	◯	◯	◯
TU	◯	◯	◯	◯
WE	◯	◯	◯	◯
TH	◯	◯	◯	◯
FR	◯	◯	◯	◯
SA	◯	◯	◯	◯
SU	◯	◯	◯	◯

21
Monday

22
Tuesday

23
Wednesday

Notes
What not to forget, what to remember

24
Thursday

25
Friday

26
Saturday

27
Sunday

MO	TU	WE	TH	FR	SA	SU
	1	2	3	4	5	6
7	8	9	10	11	12	13
14	15	16	17	18	19	20
21	22	23	24	25	26	27
28	29	30	31			

THAT'S *important* THIS *week*

MO ◯ ◯ ◯ ◯
TU ◯ ◯ ◯ ◯
WE ◯ ◯ ◯ ◯
TH ◯ ◯ ◯ ◯
FR ◯ ◯ ◯ ◯
SA ◯ ◯ ◯ ◯
SU ◯ ◯ ◯ ◯

28 Monday	**29** Tuesday	**30** Wednesday

Notes
What not to forget, what to remember

31
Thursday

Happy New Year

WELCOME 2021

Dec.
2020

MO	TU	WE	TH	FR	SA	SU
	1	2	3	4	5	6
7	8	9	10	11	12	13
14	15	16	17	18	19	20
21	22	23	24	25	26	27
28	29	30	31			

THAT'S *important* THIS *week*

MO

TU

WE

TH

FR

SA

SU

2021

January

M	T	W	T	F	S	S
				1	2	3
4	5	6	7	8	9	10
11	12	13	14	15	16	17
18	19	20	21	22	23	24
25	26	27	28	29	30	31

February

M	T	W	T	F	S	S
1	2	3	4	5	6	7
8	9	10	11	12	13	14
15	16	17	18	19	20	21
22	23	24	25	26	27	28

March

M	T	W	T	F	S	S
1	2	3	4	5	6	7
8	9	10	11	12	13	14
15	16	17	18	19	20	21
22	23	24	25	26	27	28
29	30	31				

April

M	T	W	T	F	S	S
			1	2	3	4
5	6	7	8	9	10	11
12	13	14	15	16	17	18
19	20	21	22	23	24	25
26	27	28	29	30		

May

M	T	W	T	F	S	S
					1	2
3	4	5	6	7	8	9
10	11	12	13	14	15	16
17	18	19	20	21	22	23
24	25	26	27	28	29	30
31						

June

M	T	W	T	F	S	S
	1	2	3	4	5	6
7	8	9	10	11	12	13
14	15	16	17	18	19	20
21	22	23	24	25	26	27
28	29	30				

July

M	T	W	T	F	S	S
			1	2	3	4
5	6	7	8	9	10	11
12	13	14	15	16	17	18
19	20	21	22	23	24	25
26	27	28	29	30	31	

August

M	T	W	T	F	S	S
						1
2	3	4	5	6	7	8
9	10	11	12	13	14	15
16	17	18	19	20	21	22
23	24	25	26	27	28	29
30	31					

Septembe

M	T	W	T	F	S	S
		1	2	3	4	5
6	7	8	9	10	11	12
13	14	15	16	17	18	19
20	21	22	23	24	25	26
27	28	29	30			

October

M	T	W	T	F	S	S
				1	2	3
4	5	6	7	8	9	10
11	12	13	14	15	16	17
18	19	20	21	22	23	24
25	26	27	28	29	30	31

November

M	T	W	T	F	S	S
1	2	3	4	5	6	7
8	9	10	11	12	13	14
15	16	17	18	19	20	21
22	23	24	25	26	27	28
29	30					

December

M	T	W	T	F	S	S
		1	2	3	4	5
6	7	8	9	10	11	12
13	14	15	16	17	18	19
20	21	22	23	24	25	26
27	28	29	30	31		

Space for your ideas!

www.ingramcontent.com/pod-product-compliance
Lightning Source LLC
Chambersburg PA
CBHW021422210526
45463CB00001B/493